Bucks Mills

people

Lower Bucks Mills, perched above the sea.

John Bradbeer

Introduction

The area of North Devon lying to the west of Bideford is not as well known as the coastal area stretching from Braunton to Ilfracombe and the Exmoor coast from Combe Martin to Lynton. In fact the description 'North Devon' is often taken to mean just that tract. There is no agreed name for what is really North-west Devon.

People visit Clovelly and the Hartland Peninsula but, travelling from Bideford or Barnstaple, they tend to drive directly to these places, following the A39 which skirts the large embayment known either as Barnstaple or Bideford Bay, that depending upon whether you come from Barnstaple or Bideford!

The North-west Devon countryside, through which people drive, is very appealing with deep valleys and gently rolling hills but the most impressive element of this landscape is the coast, which , in fact, is not visible at all from the A39, the 'Atlantic Highway'. At the deepest part of the embayment lies the charming village of Bucks Mills.

Bucks Mills, once a small but active fishing village, is not as well known as Clovelly, some four kilometres further west along the coast, but it has achieved some renown as the home of the Braund family, a fishing family who dominated life in the village for much of the nineteenth century.

My walk takes the visitor down through this quiet, somewhat neglected village, setting both the Braund family and its association with Bucks Mills into historic context and introducing the visitor to this fascinating little village in its beautiful coastal setting, hanging above the sea within a steep-sided, deeply wooded valley.

John Bradbeer, August 2011

L eaving the Atlantic Highway at Bucks Cross, a narrow minor road leads north dropping down through a wooded valley, until at the foot of the steepest part of the hill, the car park lies through a narrow entrance to the right. There is no other car parking available in the village. The walk starts from this car park (GR: SS358234). The walk with commentary leads eventually down to the beach, about 700 metres away. Once at the beach you may decide to return directly to this car park, although suggestions are made on ways to extend your exploration. Before setting out you may like to sit in comfort and read some background to the village and its parish connections.

Historical background

B ucks Mills lies partly in the parish of Woolfardisworthy (locally known as Woolsery, pronounced *Wools–ery*) and partly in Parkham parish, with the stream flowing down through Bucks Mills as the parish boundary. The west bank lies in Woolsery parish and the east bank within Parkham parish.

We start within Woolsery parish. The names Bucks Cross and Bucks Mills are obviously related and even the most casual visitor will have recognised Bucks Cross as being located at a crossroads with one road leading to Bucks Mills, where there must have been a mill. This is correct but not all the story.

Boc and hwisic

The Bucks part of the place names merits more attention. Until the mid-nineteenth century, it would have been written as Bucksh or even as Buckish. So it could have an apostrophe for the missing letters. It is usual to spell the name with no apostrophe. It has no associations with a person called Buck or with a male deer. Rather, it comes from two Old English words boc and hwisic. The former word means 'book' and in the context of place names means that the settlement was granted by charter. This charter also gave the right of the person granted the land to pass it on or sell without permission from the original grant-maker. The latter word (hwisic) means 'land for a family'. So we have a block of land sufficient to support a single family granted by charter.

Bucks Barton

The farmstead of this land grant is now known as Bucks Barton (GR: SS343 232), and lies 700 metres west-north-west of Bucks Cross. It gave its name to the crossroads lying within the estate and later the farm labourers' cottages opposite the farm became known as West Bucks, in that they lay west of the crossroads.

The settlement that grew up around the crossroads was at first called East Bucks and only in the nineteenth century was it referred to as Bucks Cross. Bucks was a separate manor, distinct from Woolsery by the time of the Domesday Book. It almost certainly had also acquired more land than that for the single family its name suggests, for the Domesday entry reads:

"Theobald holds Bucks himself. Three thanes held it before 1066. It paid tax for ½ hide. Land for 4 ploughs. Theobald has in lordship ½ virgate. 4 villagers. Meadow 5 acres; pasture 10 acres; underwood 20 acres. Formerly 5s; value now 12s 6d."

Hides and virgates

A hide was a variable measure of land, usually sufficient to support a single family. It was also the basis for Saxon taxation, much as the way properties used to be rated for the funding of local government until the short-lived Community Charge was brought in. Local councils levied a rate of so much per pound of rateable value. So Saxon government when seeking funds, usually to meet military expenses or to pay off the Danes with the Danegeld, would levy a payment of a fixed amount per hide of land held. The virgate is usually 30 acres or around 13 hectares. The Domesday Book uses the convention 'land for n ploughs' to indicate the potential arable land available. It was generally assumed that a plough-team could till 120 acres each year, so there would have been the potential for 480 acres (roughly 210 hectares) of arable land within the manor.

Theobald, son of Berner, is one of the smaller Domesday land-owners in Devon, with 26 manors and a house in Exeter. Most of the manors he held were sub-let but he kept Bucks for himself. About half of Theobald's manors lie in North Devon. The thanes, who held the manor before the Norman Conquest, were military servants of the king. At one time being a king's thane meant forming part of the king's body-guard, especially on the battlefield. By late Saxon times, thanes were charged with service in the local militia and attending the king should one of his royal perambulations bring him to the county.

Domesday manors

The modern parish of Woolsery contained three other Domesday manors: Woolsery itself, Almiston and Ashmansworthy, these latter two manors lying in the south-east part of the parish. These four manors together had land for 12 ploughs and included 14 villagers, 3 smallholders, and 3 slaves, with 75 acres of meadow, 50 acres of pasture, 60 cattle, 220 sheep and 20 goats. This all suggests that the manor of Bucks was a significant part of the parish and that its lands must have comprised most of its northern part. The underwood in the Domesday entry probably refers to the woods on the western side of the valley and those shrouding the cliff slopes west of the beach.

4

Three footpaths converge near the car park. This probably reflects Bucks Mills situation in two parishes, with at least one of the footpaths, once known as the Coffin Path, giving a more direct route eastwards to Parkham church.

St Anne's church, which you will have passed on your left hand side, shortly after leaving Bucks Cross, was only built in 1861, so until then, the inhabitants of Bucks Mills had to worship and bury their dead at their respective parish churches of Woolsery and Parkham, both at a distance of over six kilometres in a straight line from the village.

When you are ready to walk, leave by the path at the lower end, the north-west corner, of the car park, joining the road and heading into Bucks Mills proper. After 100 metres you will reach the old chapel of 1907 on your right.

Bursts of Revivalism

Although converted into a private dwelling house, the building is unmistakably an old chapel and the date 1907 is visible, carved above the door. This was a replacement chapel for an earlier building further into the village, now known as Leat Cottage. It is also testimony to the religious geography of North Devon in the nineteenth century.

John Wesley, the founder of Methodism, won many people to the new denomination in the late eighteenth century and, since then, there were periodic bursts of revivalism, often leading to the creation of new chapels. Indeed at Lake, outside Shebbear, some 20 km away, the preaching of one Methodist, William Bryant (or O'Brien as he liked to be called) in 1815 inspired the creation of another denomination, Bible Christianity. This became a dominant nonconformist force in North Devon, eventually merging with other Methodist groupings in 1907 and eventually reuniting with the Wesleyans and oher Methodists in 1932.

Religious rivalries

In the nineteenth century, there were often strong rivalries among various nonconformist denominations.

Fishing and agricultural labouring communities were especially touched by revivalism, with emotional preaching and the appeal to renounce alcohol seemingly striking a chord among the poorest people.

The Church of England had been slow to respond to the changing geographies of the nineteenth century, especially the development of new communities lying, as Bucks Mills does, astride ancient parish boundaries and at a distance from the medieval parish church.

So the fishing and agricultural labouring people of Bucks Cross and Bucks Mills built themselves a chapel in Bucks Mills and only in 1861 did the Elwes family, owners of the Walland estate, construct a small church for the Church of England (St Anne's).

No doubt the employees of the estate were expected to attend St Anne's but the rest of the village probably worshipped in the chapel. Indeed, local folklore has it that St Anne's was constructed to stop the Braunds of Bucks becoming 'heathens'. Heathen in this context meant that they had left the Church of England and become nonconformists.

As the nineteenth century wore on, the electoral franchise was progressively extended and another feature of North Devon's religious geography emerged; namely the association of Anglican worship with the Conservative party and of nonconformist worship with the Liberal party. This association persisted as late as the 1960s.

Walking on, Leat Cottage, the original Bucks Mills chapel, lies a further 100 metres down the road, on the left.

3 Leat Cottage

Just outside the cottage, the road bridges the stream, so you will soon cross into Woolsery parish. The water from the stream was diverted by a weir into a channel or leat that hugs the western side of the valley and more or less maintains its original height. There is no remaining sign of this weir and it was probably located some 100m further up the valley.

Looking west you can see the former course of the leat as a near horizontal line between woodland and field. The stream itself falls by several metres over the next two hundred metres. The significance of this will become clearer at the next stop.

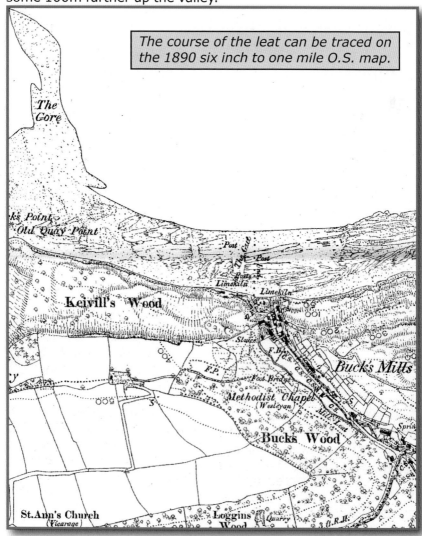

The course of the leat can be traced on the 1890 six inch to one mile O.S. map.

Continue down the road for a further two hundred metres and pause by the turning area (A) and opposite the old mill and mill house. The South West Coastal Path has come in from the right and continues up West Cliff on the left.

The old mill is now a dwelling (Mill Cottage), seen here in a photo of July 2010. The leat which gave the mill water power, followed the edge of the valley on the western side from Leat Cottage. The height difference between the leat and the stream formed the 'head' and gave the mill its power. The 1890 Six Inch map (left) shows sluices near the mill and perhaps one of the overflows can just be detected in the garden of Mill Cottage, just south of the actual building.

The mill wheel has long gone and it would have been 'undershot', that is the wheel was driven by the force of water flowing under it. North Devon seems to have had very few 'overshot' water wheels where the water plunges onto the wheel from above.

The mill owner lived in what is now called The Old Mill. This building has a plaque commemorating the Braund Society. There will be more about the Braund family at a later stop on the walk.

The mill in the nineteenth century

For much of the second half of the nineteenth century, the mill was owned by Simon Crews, who had been born in Bradworthy.

In 1871, the census records Simon, aged 40, his wife Ellen, aged 30, their two children, John (10) and Elizabeth (7) and two servants, a second Elizabeth Crews aged 12, the illegitimate daughter of Simon's sister Charlotte and William Badcock, a nephew of Simon, aged 16.

The family was still living at the mill house in 1891, having now been joined by Simon's brother William, one William Hamlyn a lodger and recorded as a sailor and Reuben Braund, aged 12 as the general servant.

The Crews family gave up the mill sometime in the 1890s and milling also ceased, possibly reflecting the decline in arable farming locally and competition from flour milled elsewhere and now more widely available, thanks to improvements in transport.

In 1908, the building was renamed the Temperance Hotel and was run as a hotel and tea shop. It continued as a tea and gift shop until the 1990s when it became again a private residence.

The Mill House in June 2010

After leaving the turning area, the path to the beach starts to steepen and on the right, just as it makes a left turn to descend the cliff, lies King's Cottage.

The king in question is James Braund. It was the custom for the senior man of the village to be called the King of Bucks, and for much of the nineteenth century, this was James Braund, or more accurately Captain James Braund, for there were other James Braunds in the village, which was soon to be associated with the Braund family name.

The 1861 census return for what is now known as King's Cottage is given below:

Name	Status	Age	Occupation	Birthplace
James Braund	Head	50	Fisherman	Parkham
Mary Braund	Wife	49	Fishing Net Weaver	Parkham
William Braund	Son	23	Fisherman	Parkham
John Braund	Son	21	Fisherman	Parkham
Elizabeth Braund	Daughter	19	Domestic Servant	Parkham
Frederick Braund	Son	17	Fisherman	Parkham
Christopher Braund	Son	15	Fisherman	Parkham
Ellen Braund	Daughter	12	Scholar	Parkham
Matilda Braund	Daughter	10	Scholar	Parkham
Reuben Braund	Son	8	Scholar	Parkham

King's Cottage

Captain James Braund

King's Cottage itself lies within Parkham parish and, no doubt, the Braund children were all born in this house. The photograph opposite is well-known and captures the spirit of this remarkable man, who finally died in 1898 at the great age of 91.

The whiskers running right around his face but with a clean shaven upper lip were characteristic of many mariners and fishermen in the late nineteenth century.

James Braund is also wearing a knitted Guernsey smock, with the extra padding on the shoulders, so that an oar could be carried more comfortably without pressing too much into the flesh.

James Braund became a pilot for Bideford Bar, guiding vessels safely through the treacherous waters at the mouth of the Taw and Torridge estuary to Appledore pool. He combined this with fishing and later became the owner and master of the smack Ebenezer.

The Ebenezer also called at other ports and beaches along the North Devon coast. James Braund also was hailed for his part in the rescue of the crew of a Clovelly herring boat in a storm in 1853.

Captain James Braund was known as the 'King of Buckish' during his lifetime was obviously seen as the senior member of the Braund family. He was 'captain' in so far as he was the master and owner of a ketch, but he would have had no other formal claim on the title.

Households named:	1851	1861	1871	1881	1891
Braund	6	6	10	12	16
Other names	19	15	15	13	13

As the table above shows, the Braunds gradually came to dominate the village of Bucks Mills. In 1841, of the 103 people recorded in the census in Bucks Mills, 33 were called Braund. By 1881, the population of the village had grown to 117 and 61 were called Braund, with several of the other families having a Braund daughter as head of the household.

There is a biography of James Braund (Janet Few) and a history of the village in the nineteenth century (Rebecca and Janet Few); see page 37. These books explain more fully the James Braund story and the complex family inter-relationships and movement of households between the houses. The very last person named Braund to live in Bucks Mills was Noel Braund who died in 1997 and, when the Powell family moved from Laburnum Cottage in 2000, the last descendants of the Braund line left the village.

Painting and Landscape

In the nineteenth century, paintings of local scenes and of fishing folk did much to popularise the sea coast away from the by now well-established resorts for sea bathing all round the coast of England. An early artist to visit Bucks Mills (1824) was JMW Turner who, from a spot close to where you now stand, painted a watercolour, 'Clovelly Bay'. This was quickly turned into an accurate etching by William Miller (Turner's favourite engraver) and published in 1826 as part of a series entitled 'Picturesque Views of the Southern Coast of England'.

The sweeping view includes distant Lundy, Gallantry Bower, Blackchurch Rock, Clovelly and, in the fore-ground, one of the Bucks Mills limekilns. In the middle distance is the Gore, here providing some shelter and a pebble bank upon which small vessels can be beached.

Peter Howard (1991) sees a distinct evolution from what he describes as romantic visions of the coast with images of dramatic sea cliffs which tended to be popular in the middle third of the nineteenth century to what he calls heroic visions that tended to portray people in their landscapes and became popular in the last third of the century. This trend was re-enforced by the new fashion for painting out of doors and English artists sought both subject matter and locations that resembled the French models of the Impressionist school.

Fishing villages and their fisherfolk were especially popular, as the rise of the Newlyn School in Cornwall attests. Although never as well known as Clovelly, Bucks Mills did have its own artist visitors and residents, especially in the twentieth century.

6   The Lookout cabin

Continuing to descend the track, beyond the King's Cottage, and, almost immediately, on the right is The Lookout cabin

The Lookout cabin, on the path down to the beach, was originally a fisherman's store but by 1913 it had been rented to Mrs Ackland, a doctor's wife from Bideford, who used it as a summer home. During the 1920s, the hut was used by her daughter Judith and her friend and companion, Mary Stella Edwards. Judith and Mary painted and made miniatures, drawing inspiration from Bucks Mills.

The Lookout cabin is upper centre of the picture, just to the right of the eastern limekiln.

The beach at Bucks Mills by Judith Ackland, painted in 1957.

In 1938 Judith took over the tenancy and, in 1948 at the sale of the Walland Cary Estate, purchased the hut. The two artists continued to use the hut until Judith's death in 1971.

The Burton Art Gallery and Museum in Bideford has a small infomative exhibition on the couple and holds a collection of Judith Ackland's paintings (see page 36).

Another of the many local artists who have turned to Bucks Mills for inspiration is the late Ken Doughty, a North Devon art teacher, who painted the beach scenes here many times.

Towards Clovelly from Bucks Mills by Ken Doughty.
Wooded cliffs here are the norm but note the raw-red scree of a recent cliff fall, a frequent occurance along this coast, but most are hidden in time by new vegetation.

It will probably not be obvious today but in March 1989 a large landslip swept away the track where you are now standing, leaving a steep scree slope spilling onto the beach.

To your left, above you, there would have been massive bare cliff-scars which threatened further falls. After extensive slope consolidation, that included clothing the slope with wire baskets of rock, the path was reopened in 1993. However, one long term consequence has been that the toilet facilities built at the foot of the path have never been reopened, since the repaired track is not considered strong enough to support the weight of the large vehicles necessary to service the facilities.

The coast to either side of Bucks Mills has seen a constant sequence of landslips, smaller slips occurring every winter. However, in the past very much bigger landslips have occurred.

The photograph on the front cover, taken at high tide on an unusually calm, fine summer evening, gives the impression of a picture postcard seashore fishing village in an idyllic setting. If, as you look down upon the beach the tide is high, then you may still have that impression but the reality, at least in the days of sail, was something very different. The sea is seldom this calm and at low tide the rocky foreshore made landing by sail hazardous. So much so that, sometime in the late eighteenth or early nineteenth century, rock ledges on the shore platform were blasted away to give a narrow gap offering a clear run into the beach for the fishing boats.

At low tide this 'Cut' or 'Gut' is plain to see. It is also shown on the 1890 six inch O.S. map on page 8, together with daymark posts placed to help to guide boats in at high tide.

Now descend the hard to the pebbles of the storm beach. There follows (topics 7 to 12), a commentary and discussion drawing attention to features best seen from the beach. These include: (7) The Gore, (8) Rocky shore and cliffs, (9) Seabirds, (10) The Waterfall and coastal change, (11) Limekilns, (12) Beach work and sailing vessels.

The beach remains the focus of Bucks Mills but now for recreation alone, compared to its use in the nineteenth century as a location for launching fishing boats and landing cargoes. There are several distinct elements of interest that can be seen from the beach that are worthy of note.

The Gore

If you have come down to the beach around low tide, you will have noticed a spit of boulders running out into the sea at right angles to the coast, about 400 metres to the west of the slipway. This is the Gore, and it extends about 200 metres into the sea. It is probable that it was the result of a massive, unrecorded cliff fall, sometime before 1795, by which time it was shown on navigation charts. The finest muddy material would have been quickly lifted into suspension and drifted out into the bay. Most of the pebble-sized debris has subsequently been moved eastwards around Bideford Bay by waves striking the shore obliquely and creating longshore drift.

The current view is that the rapid extension of the pebble ridge at Westward Ho! in the nineteenth century was the product of this cliff-fall. The Gore itself today is largely composed of boulders which were too large to be integrated into the longshore movement of debris. The Gore offers a little shelter from the north-west and so made launching and recovering boats off the beach a slightly less hazardous activity (see the Turner etching on page 14).

The Gore from the coastal cliff path

The Gore from the air. © *the Roger Chope collection*

One can appreciate the full extent of the Gore only from the air. Here, looking east along the coast, Bucks Mills is top right. The grey, cliff-foot pebbles of the storm beach, continuous from Clovelly to Westward Ho! is well defined.

A clear sea on a calm day shows the largely underwater seaward extension of the Gore, the orientation of which has been much modified by wave action.

The shoreward end of the Gore is a pleasant place to explore and gives good views back towards the cliffs but be aware that the tidal range here is high so the sea advances rapidly after low water and can cut off the unwary.

An old Pier

The beach lies at the point of the deepest embayment of Bideford Bay and is naturally sheltered from the prevailing southerly and westerly winds.

In the sixteenth century, a small stone pier, similar to that which still exists at Clovelly, was built at Bucks Mills. The pier was eventually destroyed by storms, after which some of the less massive blocks were probably incorporated in the sea wall fronting the western limekiln.

The arc of boulders in the foreground of the photo on page 18 may well be surviving foundations of the pier, close to the site labelled 'Old Quay Point' on the 1890 O.S. map.

8 A Rocky Foreshore and Cliffs

One characteristic of the cliffs along this coast is that most of the cliffs are densely wooded, often to within a few tens of metres of the sea. This is quite unusual and a reflection of the protection and shelter afforded by the Hartland peninsula against the strong prevailing winds blowing in from a west-north-west direction.

The outcrop of the rocks on the beach generally runs east to west, or parallel with the shore. The rocks have many minor folds so that sometimes the dip seems to be towards the sea and at other times away from it. This would have made it very difficult to launch a boat from this shore, until the cut was made.

This direction of the strike is also responsible for the distinctive character of the cliffs both east and west of Bucks Mills. They also have an unusual profile, termed hog's back, with a long convex slope from the coastal plateau and then a short, cliffed section, of perhaps not much more than twenty metres in height. The principal reason for this is that the strike of the rocks, or the general direction of the axes of folding, is more or less east-west and thus parallel with the coastline.

When the dip is towards the sea, the natural bedding planes in the rock strata form a sloping surface above the actual cliff face being attacked by the sea.

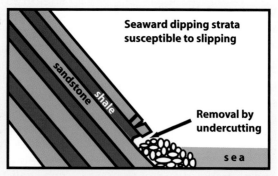

Seaward dipping strata susceptible to slipping

sandstone shale

Removal by undercutting

s e a

Here a bed of sandstone might resist the sea until it is fractured, probably along one of the major joints. The sea then cuts away a block and the whole rock face above slides down the bedding plane, exposing softer shale which is rapidly eroded by the sea. The shale band, when dampened by water seepage from higher up the cliff, also offers a well lubricated plane for slippage.

However, when the dip of the rocks is away from the sea and alternate beds of shale and sandstones occur, the sea will undercut any exposed softer shales and the massive sandstone blocks above them will topple down the cliff.

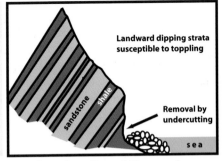

Landward dipping strata susceptible to toppling

Removal by undercutting

sandstone

shale

sea

As seen on the beach at Bucks Mills, the dip of the rocks can change very quickly from a seaward inclination to a landward inclination because of the intense folding. So both processes of slippage and toppling are occurring. The coast to either side of Bucks Mills has seen a constant sequence of landslips, smaller slips occurring every winter. As already noted, a larger than usual landslip carried away the path to the beach in 1989 and, at intervals of several centuries, really large landslips occur. The scars of these persist, detected as areas of scree.

The large landslip below, photographed in June 2009, is at Worthygate Wood (SS 365239), just one kilometre east of Bucks Mills. Here, part of the densely wooded cliff, described on the previous page, has been rafted downslope and, towards the foot of the slope, is overwhelmed by the landslip, the bulging toe of which has invaded the shore.

9 Seabirds in Bideford Bay

Another consequence of the local geology is that there are very few rock ledges suitable for nesting seabirds along the whole of the southern shore of Bideford Bay. One of the very few places where some ledges can be found is just to the east of the slipway onto the beach at Bucks Mills and in the cliff below the eastern limekiln.

Here two or three pairs of fulmars *(Fulmarus glacialis)* have nested over the last thirty or so years. The fulmars are tube-  noses, not gulls and related distantly to albatross. They can be told from gulls by their stiffer wings in flight and by their smaller size. They effectively only became common seabirds around the Bristol Channel during the twentieth century, having historically been confined to the Arctic and Britain's first fulmars were recorded from Shetland as late as 1878 (Sharrock, 1976).

Other seabirds may be observed from the beach. Herring gulls *(Larus argentatus)*, lesser black-backed gulls (*Larus fuscus*) and great black-backed gulls (*Larus marinus*) can be seen most of the year round.

Herring gull

Oystercatcher

Black and white Oystercatchers (*Haematopus ostralegus*) are frequent visitors and feed not on oysters but on mussels.

A gannet preparing to dive

A frequent visitor (left) is the shag (*Phalacrocorax aristotelis*).

In summer, gannets (*Morus bassanus*) can be seen flying low at some distance from shore. These gannets will most probably have come from the large colony on Grassholm, off the Pembrokeshire coast, some 130 kilometres away. Until the late nineteenth century there was a colony of gannets on Lundy, which can usually be seen away to the north-west. It is thought that the foghorn at the then newly built North Light on the island disturbed the birds and they have never returned to breed.

Small brown birds among the rocks and cliffs will probably be rock pipits (*Anthus petrosus*) and some breed along this stretch of the coast.

Completing the list of likely birds to see at Bucks Mills is the raven (*Corvus corax*). This very large black bird of the crow family often flies past and will sometimes be seen engaging in characteristic aerobatics, flipping over onto its back or dropping almost vertically through the air.

23

Most people seem to head on eastwards across the beach having descended the slipway. The sound of falling water may be the attraction and visitors can see that the stream which has flowed through the village now falls over the cliff beneath the eastern limekiln (see air photo, page 25).

The track passing the Lookout from King's Cottage has followed the old course of the stream, which was diverted further east to give access to the beach. The stream would have tumbled down these last twenty or thirty metres, with cataracts rather than as a single large waterfall.

But, like most of the streams between Westward Ho! and Hartland Point, its channel does not now reach the sea at current sea level. The source of the streams that converge on the car park is about 200 metres above ordnance datum.

One kilometre later, by the car park, they are just 60 metres OD. The combined stream then falls a further 20 metres to the point where it plunges over the waterfall to the beach.

Projecting the river valley profile out to sea suggests that the stream would reach modern sea level some 1.5 kilometres off-shore.

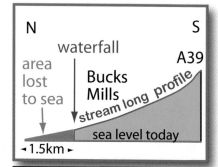

A stylized representation of the graded long profile of the Bucks Mill stream and its truncation by advancing coastal erosion.

Glacial sea levels (the last ice age peaked at about 18,000 years ago) were far lower than those of today. Indeed, the history of the last thirteen thousand years around Bideford Bay has been of a progressive rise in sea level from about 58 metres below current levels in 11,500 BC to 2 metres below current sea-level in around 50BC.

The coastline itself has changed dramatically in this period. Until about 8,800 BC Lundy was linked to the mainland and Bideford Bay would have been a gently undulating plain.

Around 6,500 BC the coast ran more or less across from Hartland Point to Morte Point, with Bucks Mills perhaps 10-12 kilometres from the sea. By around 4,400 BC, sea level was about 8 metres below present levels and the coast had more or less its current configuration but several hundred metres off-shore.

Since then we have seen the sea eating into the land. Where coastal erosion was faster than the downcutting of the local stream, its valley would gradually become more and more truncated so that, as at Bucks Mills, the valley terminates abruptly, hanging high above the beach.

Rising sea levels

Current concerns are with rising sea levels and increased storminess associated with global warming. This would seem to point to accelerating erosion of the coast, even at a relatively sheltered location such as Bucks Mills.

The Environment Agency has produced a shoreline management plan for the North Devon coast and considers that Bucks Mills should be treated as an area where there will be no active intervention to repair coastal defences or protect the cliffs in any way. The Agency feels that the infrastructure at risk from coastal erosion and flooding does not justify the level of expenditure that would be necessary to protect it. So the sea wall is patched up on a regular basis by villagers.

Bucks Mills beach at high tide from the air. Both limekilns (see following pages) are evident as is the coastal waterfall, plunging from the end of the Bucks Mills valley.

There are two limekilns at the beach, the west, lying in Woolsery parish and the east, a larger and more complex affair, which lies in Parkham parish.

The western kiln served the Walland Cary estate and is typical of the many limekilns all round the North Devon coast. Lime and coal were put into the kiln through the firing hole at ground level and the draught hole was at the top of the kiln. The kiln was charged and the lime burnt and allowed to cool before being dug out. The lime was usually slaked in water before being carted away for use on the fields.

The basic structure is much better seen at Clovelly, as the kiln on the harbour side there can be viewed when descending the cobbled High Street.

The large eastern kiln at Bucks is often mistaken for a castle and was of a different design to the western kiln. It had an inclined plane or ramp running down to the top of the kiln so that it could be recharged with coal and limestone whilst still alight.

The inclined plane has suffered from passing years and no longer reaches the kiln top. The eastern kiln was constructed about 1760.

Lime burning was a hazardous business, with temperatures needed to reduce the limestone being high and the resulting material highly caustic.

The western limekiln. Some of the large blocks in the fronting sea-wall are almost certainly derived from the ruins of the old quay at Bucks Mills.

The eastern limekiln from the path

Lime Burners

In 1861, there were three men described in the census as lime-burners, Samuel Harris, then aged 71, his son, John Harris aged 47 and John's son, also John, aged 18. It seems that Samuel Harris had learnt the skills of lime-burning at Hartland and moved to Bucks Mills at some time in the 1840s. It is also likely that people other than the Harris family helped to charge and discharge the kilns. In the 1871 census, there are no lime-burners recorded and John Harris and his son appear to have left the village, but in 1881 Samuel Baglehole who, a decade previously had been a fisherman, is described as a lime-burner.

Landing limestone & coal

For much of the nineteenth century, the trade in lime and the limekilns on the beach were a principal activity in Bucks Mills. Lime was in demand as a building material but especially for agricultural purposes.

North Devon's soils are almost everywhere acid and particularly so on the Culm Measures in the hinterland of Bucks Mills. Perhaps as early as the sixteenth century, the practice arose of importing limestone, burning it to yield quick-lime, then dousing this with water to produce slaked-lime and spreading this on the land.

The practice became particularly widespread during the eighteenth century when agricultural methods were modernised and particularly where local landlords were keen to be seen as "Improving Landowners". Most of the littoral land-owning families had at least one limekiln on their property by the mid-nineteenth century.

Although there are a few small seams of limestone in the Culm Measures, these only occur in the Lower Carboniferous in a narrow belt just south of Barnstaple and also in the Devonian rocks around Ilfracombe and Combe Martin. So, for most of North Devon, the limestone had to be imported from the Gower and South Pembrokeshire areas of South Wales.

Port records for Appledore show that much of the limestone came from Oxwich, on the Gower, and Caldey Island, just off Tenby in Pembrokeshire. Limestone quarry owners on the Gower placed adverts in the North Devon Journal during the mid-nineteenth century. Further along Bideford Bay, at Greencliff, tiny seams of Culm, a powdery anthracite, were used as fuel in the limekiln, but even there, coal had to be imported to meet the significant demand for fuel.

Pembrokeshire coalfields, rather than those in Glamorgan were the principal source of coal for North Devon's limekilns. Coal seams outcrop on the Pembrokeshire coast at Saundersfoot and on the estuary of the Cleddau (the inland tidal extension of Milford Haven). Small coastal vessels could load coal direct from the collieries at several quays on the Cleddau and from the beach at Saundersfoot. Some cargoes of coal also came from Kidwelly and Burry Port, west of Llanelli.

In the absence of a local harbour the tradition of running sailing vessels directly onto a beach was widespread and known as 'beach work'.

A very distinctive vessel developed for the limestone trade. Known as a 'polacca', a 'polacker' or a 'muffy', these were of around 50-70 tonnes and had a crew of three to five men.

The name derived from a peculiarity of the ship's mast and rigging. The main mast was a single piece of timber (see the Express left), rather than being of two parts as in most ships of the time. The first polaccas were brigs, that is, they had square sails on both masts and the technical term for them was 'hermaphrodite brig' which Devonians of the time heard, or pronounced as 'muffy'.

The fact that the main mast was a single piece of timber, a pole in effect, seems to have given rise to the name 'polacca' / 'polacker'. Later polaccas were brigantines, that is they had square sails on

Left: A polacca, the Express (of Fremington, within the Port of Barnstaple). Here she rests on a beach at Lydstep, near Tenby in Pembrokeshire, loading limestone. Note the hull profile, so suitable for lying on beaches.

the foremast but the mainsail was a large trapezoidal piece of canvas and, in mariners' parlance, was fore and aft rigged. This probably allowed the crew to be reduced in size to three men, as fore and aft sails were easier to handle.

Even before the trade began to decline in the 1870s, the polaccas were being re-rigged as ketches, two-masted vessels, with no square sails at all and still more economical to man and as seaworthy as before.

The typical polacca had very bluff bows and very round bottoms to cope with grounding on beaches. The keels and bottoms were of elm, the frames and upper planking of oak and the decks of pine. Most were built at Appledore, Barnstaple and Bideford.

Vessels with coal or lime for the limekilns at Bucks Mills were brought up the beach on a high tide and discharged into carts and panniers on the backs of horses and donkeys between tides so that on the next high tide, the ship could back off the beach and be under way again.

When is the ideal time for beach work at Bucks Mills?

On this coast, spring tides give high water from 06:00 to 10:00 and 18:00 to 22:00 (Greenwich Mean Time). So the ideal time for a ship to arrive would be on a morning spring high tide, so as to give the maximum period of daylight for discharge. If still more ideal conditions were to be sought, then it would be a spring tide around the summer solstice, with the highest tides a few days away and with an expectation of light southerly winds, to help the ship off the beach and back to sea.

Bold courage and skill

Of course, trade imperatives were such that the master could seldom wait around for such ideal conditions and had to run aground and relaunch as best he could.

The skill and daring of the masters of these vessels can only be marvelled at, particularly when there was an onshore wind making this a lee shore. Getting a vessel ship away from a lee shore is a tricky process at the best of times and absolutely impossible once the wind reaches force five or six.

The fate of a vessel so embayed, as it is called, is to be driven ashore, onto the rocks and smashed to pieces. Landing, on such a rocky shore as this, also demanded skill and good seamanship particularly with an onshore wind.

Beach work declines

The limestone trade began to fall away with the availability of cheaper alternatives. Basic slag from steel works was distributed by rail and, from the end of the nineteenth century, artificial fertilisers were also in use. The sheer physical effort involved and the low rates of pay and profit meant that the limestone trade soon died away.

An agricultural depression in the latter years of the nineteenth century also probably played its part in the decline of the trade and the growing specialisation of North Devon in livestock and dairying meant that less land was being ploughed and pasture was less often limed. Over much of North Devon in the 1840s, about 80% of the land was in some form of arable use, although the particular system employed on much of the land meant that cereals were only grown for two or three years in succession with perhaps twelve to twenty years between bouts of cereal production.

Lucy at Bucks Mills by Devon artist Michael Lees ©

This is one of a series of paintings of coastal and rural themes set within Bideford Bay, the Taw-Torridge estuary and the countryside beyond (see page 36). Below, Michael Lees comments on the particular history of this painting.

"I painted the scene over a couple of weeks in 1990 while standing on the rocks by the side of the cut. Every time the tide came in I had to grab my easel and paints and retreat up the beach. It was quite breezy so the original is ingrained with flying sand! At that time there were considerably more of the cliffs than there are now.

The Lucy and the horse were added afterwards. Trevor Davey fished from the beach and had captained one of the last sailing ketches, the Irene, and he told me about the way the sailing smacks used to sail onto the beach to unload their cargo of culm or limestone - a great skill without an engine. He approved of the painting."

(Michael Lees, March 2011)

Extending your exploration

That ends the more formal part of this walk. If you are having a picnic this might be the time to sit and ponder on the great changes this little village has seen in the last two centuries and its transformation from a working settlement to a holiday village. One enigmatic factor about Bucks Mills is the degree to which this village could ever have been described as a true 'fishing village'. The last section of the booklet examines the relationship of the village to the fishing industry.

One option now is simply to retrace your steps to the car park but if you would like a more strenuous walk, exploring the woodlands behind Bucks Mills, here are two suggestions. The O.S. Explorer Map No 126 would be useful.

1 Towards Clovelly

Climb back up the path to the turning area in front of Mill House. To the right of Mill House a guidepost indicates the Coast Path up West Hill. This is cobbled for the first few metres and then it starts to zigzag its way up through Kievell's Woods above Bucks Mills. This is a long and steep climb but through pleasant English oak and beech woodland.

After about 300 metres, another fingerpost shows the Coast Path continuing ahead, west, towards the Hobby Drive and Clovelly. The left-hand path climbs up through woodland eventually to Bucks Barton on the A39, Atlantic Highway.

2 Steart Woods - Bucks Cross

Return to the car park. Note a footpath coming in ahead and to your left. This leads along one of the streams and up through Steart Woods, to emerge on the A39, a few hundred metres to the east of Bucks Cross. The woodland you will encounter is a mixture of the regrowth of the broadleaved woodland, that has probably been here at least since medieval times, and of a more recent commercial conifer plantation. A great deal of marginal land in north-west Devon was planted with conifers, especially with sitka spruce in the 1960s. The woodlands have a typical flora and fauna and offer an interesting contrast to the coast. The path to the A39 emerges at the entrance to Steart Farm caravan park. You can return along the grass verge on the north side of the A39 to Bucks Cross and thence down the road to Bucks Mills.

Bucks Mills, as a fishing village?

Bucks Mills would seem to be a classic 'fishing village' and is certainly described as such in contemporary guides. Yet in the 1841 census, of the 24 men whose occupations are given, 12 are described as agricultural labourers and only 2 as fishermen. By 1861, fishing accounts for as many of the male labour force as agriculture and again in 1871. By 1881 only 3 men were described as fishermen, whilst 10 were described as mariners, with a further 5 households headed by women where they were described as mariner's wife. So it has to be concluded from the census returns that fishing was not the primary occupation of the people in the village.

However, what the census does not record is how many men combined some fishing with another occupation. The 1881 picture is also revealing in that about half of the village's men were mariners and may have been assumed to have learnt their seamanship, in part, as boys on the village's boats.

Pirates, legend and fact

Coastal villages were exposed to wind and waves but were also vulnerable to raiders arriving by sea. For Bucks Mills, the culmination of this exposure came in 1614, when a party of Shallee pirates landed on the beach, moving inland in search of booty and people to carry off into slavery in North Africa.

Local legend has it that Richard Cole gathered the local men and led an attack on the pirates' camp, just inland from Bucks Cross. They surprised the pirates and drove them off. Several of the fields along the road from Bucks Cross to Woolsery are called Bloody Park and, when they were ploughed in the 1960s and 1970s, often used to yield musket balls, adding some weight to the local legend. Another nearby field is called Paradise and the same folk tale has it that the local men who perished in the skirmish were buried there.

Bucks Mills and the coast of North Devon generally were always at risk of raids, especially as Lundy was frequently in the hands of pirates. Perhaps fortunately for communities such as Bucks Mills, these pirates tended to be more interested in attacking merchantmen on their way up channel to Bristol than in carrying people off into slavery.

The gradual strengthening of the British navy during the late seventeenth century reduced the threat and secured Lundy. The risk was finally eliminated by victory at Trafalgar.

A difficult market

For fishing to become a significant livelihood, there needs to be readily accessible assured markets for the fish. This was a particular limitation until the advent of refrigeration during the late nineteenth century. In effect, either fish had to be caught and delivered to their consumers within a day or salted or pickled to preserve them. By the nineteenth century, English tastes had turned against salted and pickled fish and so the only market for fish was for freshly caught fish.

Bucks Mills and Clovelly, to the west, never really overcame this handicap. Small, urban markets in Bideford and Barnstaple could be supplied and a fast schooner might be able to deliver fresh fish to the larger and more profitable market of Bristol and Bath within a day, but the volumes of fish available for sale fluctuated and in any case, there was fierce competition to supply the luxury market in Bristol/Bath.

By the 1880s, rail networks, combined with refrigeration, gave the South West's larger fishing ports, especially places like Brixham in South Devon, Newlyn in Cornwall and major national fishing ports such as Lowestoft, Yarmouth, Grimsby and Hull a decisive advantage.

Trawling?

The seabed of Bideford Bay, to the south and east of Lundy, is largely a rocky bottom and not at all suitable for trawling. There are some better areas for trawling to the west of Lundy but even these are not as extensive as those in the English Channel. So the main technological breakthrough in fishing in the early nineteenth century, the trawl, perfected by the men at Brixham and taken by them into the North Sea, was of little avail.

Long-lines could be used to take demersal (bottom-dwelling) fish, such as cod, hake, pollack and whiting but would not yield large enough volumes for other than the most local markets. Bideford Bay also has stocks of pelagic (surface-dwelling) fish. In particular, herring make an annual migration from the North Sea, through the English Channel and finally up into the Celtic Sea and the Bristol Channel.

The herring traditionally arrived in Bideford Bay in late October but, as this was at the end of a migration which itself fluctuated greatly in numbers, some years there was a glut of fish and other years there were very few fish at all. The herring were taken by drift nets, which floated in the water, well clear of any potential obstructions on the seabed. Mackerel are the other principal pelagic fish taken, either by net or on lines of spinners. As with herring, numbers fluctuate annually.

A minority occupation

All this led to fishing being a minority occupation for Bucks Mills, even if it was a very important part of the culture and tradition of the village. Fishing was always on a smaller scale in Bucks Mills than along the coast in Clovelly, where a pier allowed larger vessels to lie alongside and discharge their catches. The absence of a pier, after the loss of the sixteenth century structure, meant that Bucks Mills men had to launch their boats off the beach. Along the East Devon coast, at Beer in particular, quite large luggers between 25-28 feet (8-9 metres) long, were launched off the beach, with crews of up to five men and still more on hand to help the boat on and off the beach. Bucks Mills

never had the man-power for such large craft and its boats were around 16 to 17 feet (about 5 metres) and carvel-built (that is the planks abutted one another giving a smooth hull) and setting a small mizzen sail. It had a crew of two, often a man and a 'boy' of 12-16 years of age.

In 1952 Vernon Boyle, an indefatigable collector of information relating to North Devon ships and seafaring, wrote that Bucks Mills had a dozen such boats in the nineteenth century and this certainly would suggest that there were several part-time fishermen, not just living in Bucks Mills but also probably within half-an-hour's walk of it to give the crew of 24 necessary for all the boats.

A last fling

By the twentieth century, the Bucks Mills boat had become smaller, usually around 12 feet (or just under 4 metres), but was still carvel-built and with the advent of petrol motors, it could be sailed by one man if necessary. All the boats were built in Appledore and the last of them by boatbuilder Alan Hinks, as late as the 1960s. Gradually all the wooden craft were retired from the sea and the few boats now sporadically fishing from Bucks Mills are yet smaller and built of fibreglass.

How to count fish the North Devon way.

The late Vernon Boyle, a local historian and antiquarian, recounts the traditional way of counting fish as they were placed into baskets, called maunds.

The fisherman took three fish in his hand and these, a 'cast', were thrown into the maund. Forty such casts made a long hundred and then a further ten cast were made before a final last cast for luck. The tally came to 153 fish, the number of the miraculous draught of fishes recorded in St John's Gospel (Chapter 21 verse 11). Four tallies made a mease (pronounced may-ze).

Artists and Photographers

Whenever possible, Thematic Trails draws upon the work of local artists and photographers. John Bradbeer thanks the following for permission to reproduce illustrative work:

Michael Lees for the painting "Lucy at Bucks Mills" (page 31). A selection of paintings by Michael Lees have been published as prints and cards and can be viewed on the web site: **www.artlees.com**

Margaret Doughty for the watercolour "Towards Clovelly from Bucks Mills" (page 16) by **Ken Doughty** (1930-2009). He taught art at Barnstaple Grammar/Park School (1954-1993), one of his pupils being John Bradbeer. Exmoor and the coast of North Devon were his favourite subjects.

The Burton Art Gallery for the painting "The Beach at Bucks Mills" (page 15) by **Judith Ackland**. Amongst its wide ranging archive and displayed material, the gallery includes an "Ackland and Edwards collection". The gallery is located on the Kingsley Road, Bideford, adjacent to Victoria Park. Tel:01237-471455   Email:burtonartgallery@torridge.gov.uk **www.burtonartgallery.co.uk**

Roger Chope for the air photograph (page 19) of the Gore, from his photographic collection.

Peter Keene for the air photo on the front cover and also those on page 21 and page 25, all part of a series of air photos covering the length of the North-west Devon coast.

Unless stated otherwise all the main terrestrial photography is by **John Bradbeer**.